contents

NZ, Canada, US and UK readers
Please note that Australian cup and
spoon measurements are metric.
A conversion chart appears on page 62.

2 gluten-free for life

An allergy to gluten – the protein found in wheat – need not be a culinary millstone around your neck. With some careful research and a little forethought, delicious meals are guaranteed. But first, what does having a gluten allergy mean?

What is coeliac disease?

An extreme intolerance to gluten causes coeliac disease, a condition that is relatively common. Whenever gluten is consumed by a coeliac sufferer, it damages the lining of their small bowel (intestine). Thus, by ensuring that their diet is strictly free of gluten – for life – a sufferer of coeliac disease can live a perfectly normal, healthy existence. Recognising the symptoms of coeliac disease, however, can be a little tricky, as the effects on different Coeliacs vary markedly. Sufferers are born with the condition but, while some infants quickly become seriously ill, others develop problems slowly over a period of several years. Currently, a large percentage of newly diagnosed Coeliacs are actually adults.

It is imperative that you seek medical advice in order to receive a correct diagnosis.

Recognising the symptoms

The most common symptoms experienced by adults include:

- diarrhoea
- fatigue, weakness and lethargy
- anaemia – an iron or folic acid deficiency is most common
- weight loss
- constipation
- flatulence and abdominal distension
- cramping and bloating
- nausea and vomiting.

What foods should I avoid?

All wheat products should be avoided at all costs, so anything containing wheat flour, such as ordinary bread, biscuits, cakes, pastries, puddings, pies and pasta, is off limits. So, too, is couscous, burghul, some sauces and gravies, stuffing mixes and even sausages. Proteins similar to gluten are also found in rye, barley, triticale and oats, so any foods containing these products are also out of bounds. Gluten is also contained in manufactured and processed foods, where wheat flour is used as a binder or filler, or as a carrier for flavourings and spices. If you plan on starting a gluten-free diet, it is essential that you first consult with a qualified dietitian so that, acting under their advice, you can become ingredient-aware. If you are not sure of the gluten content of any food, follow the general rule: if in doubt, leave it out!

So what can I eat?

Having to follow a gluten-free diet may seem limiting, but the list of tasty, fresh foods that are naturally devoid of gluten is long. All fresh meat, fish, rice, cheese, eggs, milk, fruit and vegetables are perfectly okay to eat, as is a wide variety of "alternatives". Special gluten-free breads are available, and potato flour, arrowroot, cornflour, buckwheat flour, soy flour, ground rice flour and chickpea flour (besan) are all good substitutes for wheat flour. To obtain an informative list of ingredients and their suitability to a gluten-free diet, contact The Coeliac Society in your state.

4 rice moussaka

You will need about 1/2 cup uncooked short-grain rice.

1 large eggplant (500g)

2 tablespoons olive oil

1 clove garlic, crushed

3 green onions, chopped finely

100g button mushrooms, sliced finely

2 tablespoons dry white wine

400g can tomatoes

2 teaspoons tomato paste

1/2 teaspoon ground cinnamon

1 teaspoon sugar

2 tablespoons finely chopped fresh flat-leaf parsley

1 1/2 cups cooked short-grain white rice

2 tablespoons finely grated parmesan cheese

1/2 teaspoon ground nutmeg

sauce

60g butter

1/3 cup (50g) 100% corn cornflour

1 1/3 cups (330ml) milk

1/2 cup (125ml) cream

2 tablespoons finely grated parmesan cheese

1 egg yolk

Cut eggplant into 5mm slices. Place eggplant in strainer, sprinkle with salt; stand 30 minutes. Rinse eggplant under cold water; drain on absorbent paper. Place eggplant slices in single layer on oven trays, brush with half of the oil; grill on both sides until browned lightly, drain.

Heat remaining oil in large saucepan; cook garlic, onion and mushrooms, stirring, until onion is soft. Add wine; cook, uncovered, until liquid has evaporated. Add undrained crushed tomatoes, paste, cinnamon, sugar and parsley; simmer, uncovered, until thickened slightly. Stir in rice and cheese.

Oil 1.5-litre (6-cup) ovenproof dish. Place one-third of the eggplant slices over base of prepared dish, top with half of the rice mixture; then half of the remaining eggplant, remaining rice mixture and remaining eggplant. Spread Sauce over eggplant, sprinkle with nutmeg. Bake, uncovered, in moderate oven about 30 minutes or until browned lightly.

Sauce Melt butter in medium saucepan. Add cornflour; cook, stirring, until mixture thickens and bubbles. Gradually stir in milk and cream; stir until sauce boils and thickens. Remove from heat; stir in cheese and egg yolk.

4 (680g) single chicken breast fillets

100% corn cornflour

1 egg, beaten lightly

1 tablespoon whole egg mayonnaise

1 tablespoon water

1½ cups (250g) polenta

1 tablespoon chopped fresh oregano leaves

vegetable oil, for shallow-frying

lemon buttered zucchini

3 medium zucchini (360g)

60g butter

1 medium brown onion (150g), sliced

1 clove garlic, crushed

1½ tablespoons lemon juice

Place chicken between sheets of plastic wrap, gently pound until 1cm thick. Toss chicken in cornflour, shake off excess. Dip chicken into combined egg, mayonnaise and water; then coat in combined polenta and oregano, pressing coating on firmly.

Shallow-fry chicken, in hot oil, until browned lightly both sides and cooked through; drain on absorbent paper. Serve with Lemon Buttered Zucchini.

Lemon Buttered Zucchini Using vegetable peeler, cut zucchini into long strips. Melt butter in medium saucepan; cook onion and garlic, stirring, until onion is soft. Add zucchini; cook, stirring, until zucchini is just soft, stir in juice.

special bread

1 cup (150g) rice flour

¹/₃ cup (40g) soy flour

1¹/₂ teaspoons gluten-free baking powder

1 cup (250ml) milk

1 egg, beaten lightly

1 teaspoon margarine

Sift flours and baking powder into medium bowl, make a well in centre, add combined milk and egg; whisk until batter is well combined.

Melt margarine in 24cm non-stick frying pan. Pour batter into pan; cook, covered, over low heat until surface becomes dry, turn and cook until browned underneath, cool.

Cut bread into quarters, then split and use for sandwiches.

allergy-free # pizza

2 medium red capsicums (400g)

2 cloves garlic, quartered

1 tablespoon olive oil

1 medium brown onion (150g), sliced finely

2 bacon rashers, chopped roughly

1/2 cup fresh basil leaves, shredded finely

2 medium zucchini (240g), sliced finely

200g firm tofu, grated coarsely

pizza base

3/4 cup (110g) rice flour

1/2 cup (85g) polenta

1/2 cup (75g) potato flour

1/4 cup (60ml) olive oil

2/3 cup (160ml) warm water

Press Pizza Base over oiled 31cm pizza pan. Quarter capsicums, remove and discard seeds and membranes. Roast under grill or in very hot oven, skin-side up, until skin blisters and blackens. Cover capsicum pieces in plastic or paper for 5 minutes, peel away skin, chop capsicum roughly. Blend or process capsicum and garlic until smooth; spread over Pizza Base.

Heat oil in medium saucepan; cook onion and bacon, stirring, until onion is soft and browned lightly. Sprinkle half of the basil over pizza base, top with onion mixture, zucchini and tofu; sprinkle with remaining basil.

Bake, uncovered, in moderately hot oven about 20 minutes or until browned.

Pizza Base Sift dry ingredients into medium bowl, gradually stir in combined oil and water; mix to a soft dough. Turn dough onto surface lightly dusted with rice flour; knead until smooth.

3 cups (450g) gluten-free plain flour

1¼ cups (185g) buckwheat flour

2 teaspoons gluten-free baking powder

1½ teaspoons salt

70g butter

1 cup (160g) sunflower seed kernels

1½ cups (375ml) milk

2 eggs, beaten lightly

2 teaspoons poppy seeds

Sift flours, baking powder and salt into large bowl. Rub in butter. Stir in kernels, combined milk and eggs; do not overmix. Press mixture into oiled 14cm x 21cm loaf pan; do not smooth top. Brush with a little extra milk, sprinkle with seeds. **Bake** in moderate oven about 1 hour. Stand bread 10 minutes before turning onto wire rack to cool.

chocolate
cake

You will need
1 large overripe
banana (230g).

1 cup (125g) soy flour

3/4 cup (110g) 100%
corn cornflour

1 1/4 teaspoons
bicarbonate of soda

1/2 cup (50g)
cocoa powder

1 1/4 cups (275g)
caster sugar

150g butter, melted

1 tablespoon
white vinegar

1 cup (250ml)
evaporated milk

2 eggs

1/2 cup mashed banana

2 tablespoons
raspberry jam

Grease two 22cm round sandwich cake pans,
line bases with baking paper.
Sift flours, soda, cocoa and sugar into large
bowl; add butter, vinegar and milk. Beat with
electric mixer on low speed 1 minute; add
eggs, banana and jam, beat on medium speed
2 minutes. Pour cake mixture into prepared
pans; bake in moderate oven about 30 minutes.
Stand cakes in pans 5 minutes; turn onto wire
racks to cool.
Sandwich cakes with whipped cream, if desired.

tandoori lamb with

indian rice seasoning

You will need about 1/3 cup uncooked basmati rice.

2 teaspoons vegetable oil

1 small white onion (80g), chopped finely

1 clove garlic, crushed

2 teaspoons black mustard seeds

2 teaspoons cumin seeds

1 teaspoon ground coriander

1 cup cooked basmati rice

1/3 cup (30g) stale gluten-free breadcrumbs

1 egg, beaten lightly

1 tablespoon lemon juice

1.25kg boned lamb shoulder

1/2 cup (125ml) pure cultured yogurt

2 tablespoons tandoori paste

Heat oil in medium saucepan; cook onion and garlic, stirring, until onion is soft. Add seeds and coriander; cook, stirring, until seeds begin to pop. Combine spice mixture in medium bowl with rice, breadcrumbs, egg and juice.

Fill cavity of lamb with rice seasoning; roll to enclose filling, tie with kitchen string. Brush lamb with combined yogurt and paste; place in oiled baking dish. Roast, uncovered, in moderate oven about 1½ hours or until cooked as desired. Remove from heat, cover; stand 10 minutes before slicing and serving.

meatballs, ratatouille and
ricotta rice cake

You will need about 2 tablespoons of uncooked long-grain rice.

500g minced beef

1 small brown onion (80g), chopped finely

2 cloves garlic, crushed

1 tablespoon tomato paste

1 teaspoon ground coriander

1/3 cup (30g) stale gluten-free breadcrumbs

1/2 teaspoon finely grated lemon rind

2 tablespoons olive oil

ratatouille

2 tablespoons olive oil

1 large brown onion (200g), sliced thickly

2 cloves garlic, crushed

1 medium green capsicum (200g), chopped coarsely

1 medium zucchini (120g), chopped coarsely

1 finger eggplant (60g), chopped coarsely

2 tablespoons tomato paste

400g can tomatoes

1/2 cup (125ml) vegetable stock

ricotta rice cake

1 tablespoon polenta

2 cups (400g) ricotta cheese

1/4 cup (20g) finely grated parmesan cheese

1/2 cup cooked long-grain white rice

1 egg, separated

1 tablespoon finely shredded fresh basil leaves

Combine beef, onion, garlic, paste, coriander, breadcrumbs and rind in large bowl; mix well. Using wet hands, roll level tablespoons of beef mixture into balls; place on tray.

Heat oil in large non-stick frying pan; cook meatballs, in batches, until browned all over and cooked through; drain on absorbent paper. Serve Meatballs with Ratatouille and Ricotta Rice Cake.

Ratatouille Heat oil in large saucepan; cook onion and garlic, stirring, until onion is soft. Add capsicum, zucchini and eggplant; cook, stirring, until vegetables are soft. Add paste, undrained crushed tomatoes and stock; simmer, uncovered, about 10 minutes or until sauce thickens.

Ricotta Rice Cake Oil base and side of 20cm round sandwich cake pan; line base with foil, oil the foil. Sprinkle polenta over base and side of prepared pan. Combine ricotta, parmesan, rice, egg yolk and basil in large bowl; mix well. Whisk egg white in small bowl until soft peaks form; fold egg white through cheese mixture. Spread into prepared pan; bake, uncovered, in moderately hot oven about 30 minutes or until firm. Cool 5 minutes before cutting into wedges.

14 fish with spicy
polenta batter

1 cup (150g)
brown rice flour

*1/2 teaspoon gluten-free
baking powder*

1 teaspoon
ground cumin

1 teaspoon
ground coriander

*1/4 teaspoon
chilli powder*

1/3 cup (55g) polenta

3/4 cup (180ml) water

3/4 cup (180ml) coconut milk

600g small white fish fillets

extra brown rice flour

vegetable oil, for deep-frying

Sift flour, baking powder and spices
into medium bowl, stir in polenta;
gradually beat in combined water and
milk, mix to a smooth batter (or blend or
process all ingredients until smooth).
Toss fish in extra flour, shake off
excess; dip into batter. Deep-fry,
in batches, in hot oil, until browned
and cooked through; drain on
absorbent paper.

tuna mornay

*You will need about
1/3 cup of uncooked
long-grain brown rice.*
3/4 cup cooked long-
grain brown rice

1/4 medium green
capsicum (50g),
chopped finely

30g butter

1 medium brown
onion (150g),
chopped finely

1 trimmed stick
celery (75g),
chopped finely

1 1/2 tablespoons
100% corn cornflour

1 1/4 cups (310ml) milk

425g can tuna in
brine, drained, flaked

1 teaspoon finely
grated lemon rind

2 tablespoons
lemon juice

1 1/2 cups (50g) puffed
rice, crushed

40g butter,
melted, extra

1 tablespoon finely
chopped fresh
flat-leaf parsley

Combine rice and capsicum in medium bowl;
spoon mixture into base of four 1-cup (250ml)
ovenproof dishes.
Melt butter in medium saucepan; cook onion
and celery, stirring, until onion is soft. Add
cornflour; cook, stirring, until mixture thickens
and bubbles. Gradually stir in milk; stir until
mixture boils and thickens. Remove from heat;
stir in tuna, rind and juice.
Spoon mixture into prepared dishes; sprinkle
with combined puffed rice, extra butter and
parsley. Bake, uncovered, in moderate oven
about 15 minutes or until heated through.

16 sticky chicken with
garlic rice and asian coleslaw

1/2 teaspoon chilli powder

1 tablespoon ground cumin

1 tablespoon ground coriander

1/3 cup (80ml) honey

1 clove garlic, crushed

8 (680g) chicken wings

4 (600g) chicken drumsticks

garlic rice

1 cup (200g) long-grain white rice

10g butter

1 clove garlic, crushed

1 tablespoon finely chopped fresh flat-leaf parsley

asian coleslaw

1/2 medium Chinese cabbage (300g), shredded finely

1 medium carrot (120g), grated coarsely

3 green onions, sliced

1/4 cup (60ml) wheat-free tamari

1 teaspoon sugar

Heat small frying pan, add spices; cook, stirring, until fragrant. Stir in honey and garlic. Brush warm honey mixture over chicken in lightly oiled baking dish. Bake, uncovered, in moderate oven about 40 minutes or until chicken is cooked through. Brush chicken occasionally with pan juices during cooking.

Serve chicken with Garlic Rice and Asian Coleslaw.

Garlic Rice Cook rice in large saucepan of boiling water, uncovered, until tender; drain. Return rice to pan, add butter, garlic and parsley; stir until butter is melted.

Asian Coleslaw Combine ingredients in large bowl.

fish and rice patties
with chilli sauce

You will need about ¹/₂ cup of uncooked long-grain rice.

500g boneless white fish fillets, chopped

¹/₄ cup firmly packed fresh coriander leaves

2 tablespoons chopped fresh lemon grass

2 cloves garlic, crushed

1 tablespoon sweet chilli sauce

2 teaspoons fish sauce

1¹/₃ cups cooked long-grain white rice

cooking-oil spray

chilli sauce

¹/₄ cup (60ml) sweet chilli sauce

1¹/₂ tablespoons water

1 tablespoon lime juice

Process fish, coriander, lemon grass, garlic and sauces until well combined. Add half of the rice; process until just combined.

Transfer mixture to medium bowl, stir in remaining rice. Using wet hands, shape mixture into 12 patties. Place patties on baking-paper-lined oven trays; cover, refrigerate 1 hour.

Coat patties with oil spray; bake, uncovered, in moderately hot oven about 15 minutes or until cooked through. Serve patties with Chilli Sauce.

Chilli Sauce Combine ingredients in screw-top jar; shake well.

crustless vegetable
quiche

1 medium kumara (400g), chopped coarsely

1 large red capsicum (350g)

2 teaspoons olive oil

1 large red onion (300g), sliced thinly

2 cloves garlic, crushed

2 small zucchini (180g), sliced finely

⅓ cup finely chopped fresh flat-leaf parsley

250g spinach, shredded

⅓ cup (40g) seeded black olives, halved

200g fetta cheese, chopped

½ cup (125ml) light sour cream

½ cup (125ml) skim milk

4 eggs, beaten lightly

Boil, steam or microwave kumara until tender; cool. Quarter capsicum, remove and discard seeds and membranes. Roast under grill or in very hot oven, skin-side up, until skin blisters and blackens. Cover capsicum pieces in plastic or paper for 5 minutes, peel away skin, cut capsicum into thin strips.

Heat oil in large frying pan; cook onion, garlic and zucchini, stirring, until zucchini is tender. Add parsley and spinach; cook, stirring, until spinach is just wilted. Combine spinach mixture with kumara, capsicum, olives and cheese in large bowl; spoon into oiled shallow 26cm ovenproof flan dish. Pour over combined cream, milk and eggs. Bake, uncovered, in moderate oven about 45 minutes or until set.

coconut prawn burgers
with mango salsa

³/₄ cup (150g) calrose white rice

1²/₃ cups (410ml) coconut cream

¹/₂ cup (125ml) water

1kg medium uncooked prawns

1 tablespoon red curry paste

1 egg, beaten lightly

¹/₃ cup (50g) rice flour

2 large mangoes (1.2kg), chopped finely

1 small red onion (100g), chopped finely

¹/₄ cup finely chopped fresh coriander leaves

¹/₄ cup (60ml) lime juice

Combine rice, coconut cream and water in medium saucepan. Bring to a boil; simmer, covered tightly, about 15 minutes or until rice is tender and liquid absorbed.

Shell and devein prawns; discard heads and tails. Chop prawn meat coarsely; combine in medium bowl with rice mixture, paste, egg and flour. Cover; refrigerate 30 minutes.

Shape prawn mixture into 12 patties; cook, in batches, in large heated oiled frying pan until browned both sides and cooked through. Drain on absorbent paper.

Meanwhile, combine remaining ingredients in small bowl; serve salsa with prawn burgers.

20 onion polenta with
warm bean salad

8 large egg tomatoes
(720g), halved

2 tablespoons vegetable oil

4 medium brown onions (600g),
sliced thinly

2 tablespoons sugar

2 cups (500ml) milk

3¹/₂ cups (875ml) water

1 large gluten-free chicken
stock cube

1¹/₂ cups (250g) polenta

¹/₂ cup (125ml) cream

2 cloves garlic, crushed

warm bean salad

400g green beans,
chopped roughly

1 tablespoon vegetable oil

1 tablespoon lemon juice

2 birdseye chillies, seeded,
chopped finely

2 teaspoons finely chopped
fresh flat-leaf parsley

Grease a 22cm round springform tin, cover base with baking paper.
Place tomatoes, cut-side up, in baking dish; drizzle with half of the oil. Bake, uncovered, in very hot oven about 30 minutes or until soft.
Heat remaining oil in large saucepan; cook onion, stirring, until soft. Add sugar; cook, stirring occasionally, until onion is very soft and browned.
Bring combined milk, water and crumbled stock cube to a boil in large saucepan; gradually add polenta, simmer, stirring, about 10 minutes or until polenta thickens. Stir in cream and garlic. Spread polenta into prepared tin, top with caramelised onion and tomatoes.
Bake, uncovered, in hot oven about 15 minutes or until hot.
Stand 10 minutes before serving with Warm Bean Salad.
Warm Bean Salad Boil, steam or microwave beans until just tender; drain. Combine beans with oil, juice, chilli and parsley in bowl.

french meringues
with berries

Beat egg whites and juice in small bowl with electric mixer until soft peaks form. Add sugar, in batches, beating until dissolved between additions.
Line three oven trays with baking paper, trace twelve 5.5cm circles onto each sheet of baking paper. Spread meringue thinly over circles on paper, sprinkle with nuts; bake in very slow oven about 30 minutes or until crisp. Cool in oven with door ajar.
Divide Fruche among 18 of the meringues, top with raspberries and blueberries; top with remaining meringues. Top with extra berries, if desired.

2 egg whites

1 teaspoon lemon juice

½ cup (110g) caster sugar

⅓ cup (50g) shelled pistachios, chopped

200g tub low-fat strawberry Fruche

75g fresh raspberries

75g fresh blueberries

Makes 18

cantonese-style
deep-fried chicken

You will need about 1¹/₃ cups uncooked jasmine rice.

750g single chicken breast fillets

1 tablespoon wheat-free tamari

1 tablespoon sweet chilli sauce

2 cloves garlic, crushed

2 teaspoons grated fresh ginger

1 egg, beaten lightly

¹/₂ cup (75g) rice flour

vegetable oil, for deep-frying

chilli rice

4 cups cooked hot jasmine rice

4 green onions, chopped finely

1 Lebanese cucumber (130g), chopped finely

2 tablespoons sweet chilli sauce

Cut chicken into 3cm strips. Combine chicken, sauces, garlic and ginger in large bowl. Cover, refrigerate 3 hours or overnight.

Add egg to chicken mixture, stir in flour. Deep-fry chicken pieces, in batches, in hot oil, until browned and cooked through. Do not have oil too hot or chicken will overbrown before cooking through. Serve with Chilli Rice.

Chilli Rice Combine ingredients in large bowl; mix well.

24 minted lamb and vermicelli soup

100g rice vermicelli

2 tablespoons peanut oil

1kg lamb fillets, sliced

2 teaspoons sambal oelek

2 tablespoons finely chopped fresh lemon grass

2 tablespoons grated fresh ginger

4 cloves garlic, crushed

⅓ cup (80ml) fish sauce

1.5 litres (6 cups) chicken stock

1 tablespoon sugar

500g asparagus, chopped coarsely

¼ cup finely chopped fresh coriander leaves

⅓ cup finely chopped fresh mint leaves

8 green onions, chopped finely

4 medium tomatoes (760g), seeded, sliced

Place vermicelli in medium heatproof bowl, cover with boiling water, stand only until just tender; drain.

Heat half of the oil in large saucepan; cook lamb, in batches, until browned all over. Heat remaining oil in same pan; cook sambal, lemon grass, ginger and garlic, stirring, until fragrant. Add sauce, stock and sugar; bring to a boil. Add asparagus; simmer, uncovered, until asparagus is just tender. Stir in herbs, onion, tomato, noodles and lamb; stir until hot.

chicken and basil
omelette rolls

1 tablespoon olive oil

9 eggs

3 green onions,
chopped finely

1/3 cup (50g) drained
sun-dried tomatoes in
oil, sliced thinly

1½ cups (250g) finely
chopped cooked chicken

1½ cups (185g) coarsely
grated cheddar cheese

2 tablespoons chopped
fresh basil leaves

Heat a little of the oil
in large non-stick frying
pan. Lightly beat 3 of
the eggs in small bowl,
pour into pan; cook until
set underneath.
Place one-third of the
remaining ingredients
in centre of omelette;
cook about 1 minute
or until heated through.
Slide omelette from
pan, roll up; cut into
four slices. Repeat with
remaining ingredients.

26

bubble and
squeak <small>pie</small>

This is a delicious way of making a meal out of leftover vegetables.
For this recipe, you will need five cooked tiny new potatoes,
one 200g piece cooked pumpkin and one medium cooked carrot.

2 teaspoons vegetable oil

1 large brown onion (200g),
chopped coarsely

2 cloves garlic, crushed

500g minced beef

2 tablespoons tomato sauce

1 tablespoons tamari

1 cup (250ml) beef stock

1 cup (165g) cooked
corn kernels

1 cup (180g) coarsely
chopped cooked potatoes

1 cup (160g) coarsely
chopped cooked pumpkin

1/2 cup (100g) coarsely
chopped cooked carrot

1 cup cooked peas (140g)

1/4 cup (30g) coarsely
grated cheddar cheese

topping

1 large (300g) potato,
chopped coarsely

300g pumpkin, chopped

40g butter

1/4 cup (30g) coarsely
grated cheddar cheese

Heat oil in large saucepan; cook onion and garlic, stirring, until onion is soft. Add beef; cook, stirring, until well browned. Stir in sauces tamari and stock; bring to a boil. Simmer, covered, 20 minutes. Add corn, potato, pumpkin, carrot and peas; mix well.

Spoon beef mixture into shallow 2-litre (8-cup) oiled ovenproof baking dish. Spread Topping over beef mixture; sprinkle with cheese. Bake, uncovered, in moderately hot oven about 30 minutes or until browned and hot.

Topping Boil, steam or microwave potato and pumpkin until tender; drain. Place potato and pumpkin in medium saucepan; mash over low heat until smooth. Stir in butter and cheese; cook, stirring, until butter and cheese melt and mixture is smooth.

rice-stick-crusted chicken
with garlic mash

100g dried rice stick noodles

4 (680g) single chicken breast fillets

rice flour

2 eggs, beaten lightly

1 teaspoon hot paprika

1/2 large gluten-free chicken stock cube

1 clove garlic, crushed

4 green onions, chopped finely

1/4 cup (60ml) olive oil

5 medium potatoes (1kg), chopped

2 cloves garlic, crushed, extra

1/3 cup (25g) coarsely grated parmesan cheese

1/2 cup (125ml) buttermilk

1 tablespoon finely grated lemon rind

1 tablespoon finely chopped fresh flat-leaf parsley

Place noodles in large heatproof bowl, cover with boiling water, stand until just tender; drain.

Pound chicken fillets until an even thickness. Toss chicken in flour, shake off excess. Dip chicken into egg, then coat in combined noodles, paprika, crumbled stock cube, garlic and onion.

Heat oil in large frying pan; cook chicken until browned both sides and cooked through. Remove chicken; cover to keep warm.

Meanwhile, boil, steam or microwave potato until tender; drain. Mash potato in large bowl with extra garlic, cheese and buttermilk.

Sprinkle chicken with combined lemon rind and parsley; serve with garlic mash.

spiced chicken

with rice seasoning

1.5kg chicken

1 tablespoon peanut oil

2 teaspoons
ground cumin

2 tablespoons gluten-
free mild curry powder

1 teaspoon
garlic powder

rice seasoning

1 tablespoon peanut oil

1 medium brown onion
(150g), chopped finely

1 clove garlic, crushed

1 teaspoon
ground cumin

1 teaspoon
ground turmeric

1/2 cup (100g) short-
grain white rice

1 cup (250ml) water

1 large gluten-free
chicken stock cube

1/4 cup (35g)
dried currants

1/4 cup (35g) slivered
almonds, toasted

1 tablespoon finely
chopped fresh
coriander leaves

Fill cavity of chicken with Rice Seasoning,
secure openings with toothpicks. Tie legs
together, tuck wings under body. Place
chicken on wire rack over baking dish, rub with
combined oil, cumin, curry powder and garlic
powder. Bake, uncovered, in moderate oven
about 1 1/2 hours or until chicken is cooked
through. Brush chicken occasionally with its
pan juices during cooking.

Rice Seasoning Heat oil in medium heavy-
base saucepan; cook onion, garlic, cumin and
turmeric, stirring, until onion is soft. Add rice;
stir until coated with oil. Stir in the water and
crumbled stock cube; stir over heat until mixture
boils. Cover with tight-fitting lid; simmer
12 minutes. Remove from heat, stand, covered,
10 minutes. Stir in remaining ingredients;
cool 10 minutes before filling chicken.

vietnamese
beef noodle soup

2 birdseye chillies

1 tablespoon
peanut oil

1 large brown onion
(200g), chopped

2 cloves garlic,
crushed

1 medium carrot
(120g), chopped

1 tablespoon grated
fresh ginger

1 litre (4 cups)
beef stock

2 cups (500ml) water

1 teaspoon black
peppercorns

2 star anise

1 tablespoon
fish sauce

500g beef rump steak,
sliced thinly

400g fresh rice
noodles

120g bean sprouts

3 green onions,
sliced thickly

2 tablespoons fresh
mint leaves

1/2 medium lemon
(70g), quartered

Remove seeds and membranes from chillies;
cut lengthways into thin strips.
Heat oil in large saucepan; cook onion, garlic,
carrot and ginger, stirring, until onion is soft. Stir
in stock, water, pepper, star anise and sauce.
Bring to a boil; simmer, uncovered, 30 minutes.
Strain stock mixture through two pieces of
muslin into large saucepan; discard vegetables
and muslin. Bring stock to a boil.
Meanwhile, divide chilli, beef, noodles, sprouts,
onion, mint and lemon among serving bowls;
ladle in boiling stock.

200g dark chocolate, chopped

30g unsalted butter

3 eggs, separated

300ml carton thickened cream, whipped

Place chocolate in heatproof bowl, place over pan of simmering water; stir chocolate until melted, remove from heat. Add butter, stir until melted; stir in egg yolks one at a time. Transfer mixture to large bowl, cover; cool.

Beat egg whites in small bowl with electric mixer until soft peaks form. Fold cream and egg whites into chocolate mixture in two batches.

Pour into 12 serving dishes (1/3-cup capacity); refrigerate several hours or overnight.

Serve with extra whipped cream and chocolate curls, if desired.

Serves 12

An allergy to gluten is no reason to miss out on delectable breads, gooey cakes and tasty noodles. Read on for a selection of alternatives to foods that you can't otherwise eat.

Fresh rice noodles are thick, wide and almost white in colour, and are made from rice and vegetable oil. Delicious in soups and stir-fries, fresh rice noodles must be covered with boiling water to remove starch and excess oil before using. Incorporated into a gluten-free diet, fresh rice noodles can also serve as a scrumptious substitute for pasta and wheat flour noodles.

Rice vermicelli is also known as rice-flour noodles, and is made from ground rice. Widely available in supermarkets, rice vermicelli is sold dried, in packets, and is best either deep-fried or soaked, then stir-fried or used in soups.

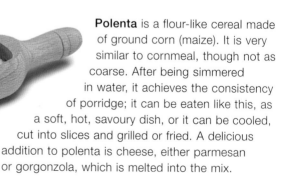

Polenta is a flour-like cereal made of ground corn (maize). It is very similar to cornmeal, though not as coarse. After being simmered in water, it achieves the consistency of porridge; it can be eaten like this, as a soft, hot, savoury dish, or it can be cooled, cut into slices and grilled or fried. A delicious addition to polenta is cheese, either parmesan or gorgonzola, which is melted into the mix.

Corn tortillas are flat, round, unleavened bread – resembling very thin pancakes – which are a tasty, easy bread alternative for those with gluten allergies. After a tortilla is baked on a griddle, it can be eaten plain or wrapped around various fillings. Tortillas are the basis of several famous Mexican delights: tacos, burritos and enchiladas. Corn tortillas are available in most supermarkets.

Flours:

These flours are available at most good health food stores.

Soy: A creamy flour processed from soy beans, soy flour can be used in batters.

Potato: This white powder, made from potatoes, is perfect to thicken soups and sauces, and is also used in cakes and biscuits (especially in Jewish and European cooking).

Rice: Flour ground from rice grains, rice flour is used to make rice noodles, as a thickener, and in combination with other flours for cakes, shortbread and biscuits.

Chickpea (besan or gram): This heavy, finely milled flour, made from dried chickpeas, has a pleasing flavour and is used in batters, doughs and pastries.

Buckwheat: A flour milled and processed from the triangular seeds of an annual plant, and used in blini (pancakes) and in buckwheat noodles (check labels before buying noodles as they can be made with a combination of buckwheat flour and wheat flour).

Tapioca: A starch extracted from the roots of a shrub, tapioca flour is used to bake a variety of breads and cakes. Granulated or pearled tapioca can be used in stews and soups as a thickener.

Cornflour (maize): A fine white powder extracted from maize (corn), cornflour is used mainly as a thickener for sauces and pie fillings, and for baking cakes. Be careful not to mistakenly use wheaten cornflour, which does contain gluten.

chicken spinach
lasagne

Fresh rice noodle sheets, on average, measure 40cm x 70cm when unfolded; there are usually 2 sheets to a 1kg package. They don't need pre-cooking for this recipe.

2 tablespoons olive oil

6 (1kg) single chicken breast fillets

2 medium brown onions (300g), sliced thinly

2 cloves garlic, crushed

200g button mushrooms, sliced

500g spinach, trimmed

100g butter

1/2 cup (75g) 100% corn cornflour

2 1/2 cups (625ml) milk

1/4 cup (60ml) dry white wine

1 egg yolk

1/2 cup (40g) coarsely grated romano cheese

500g fresh rice noodle sheet

Heat half of the oil in large saucepan; cook chicken, in batches, until browned both sides and cooked through. Cover; stand 5 minutes. Cut into 1cm slices.

Add onion and garlic to same pan; cook, stirring, until onion is just soft. Remove from pan.

Heat remaining oil in same pan; cook mushrooms, stirring, until just soft. Drain on absorbent paper.

Boil, steam or microwave spinach until wilted; rinse under cold water. Press out excess liquid; drain on absorbent paper.

Melt butter in medium saucepan. Add cornflour; cook, stirring, until mixture thickens and bubbles. Gradually stir in milk and wine; stir until sauce boils and thickens. Remove from heat; stir egg yolk and half of the cheese into white sauce.

Cut noodle sheet into nine pieces, each measuring 12cm x 16cm. Place three noodle pieces over base of oiled 2.5-litre (10-cup) ovenproof dish. Spread half of the chicken, spinach, onion mixture and mushrooms over noodles; cover with three noodle pieces and half of the white sauce. Repeat layering with remaining chicken, spinach, onion mixture and mushrooms, finishing with the last three noodle pieces. Pour remaining white sauce over noodles, sprinkle with remaining cheese.

Bake, uncovered, in moderate oven about 45 minutes or until top is browned.

leek, prosciutto
and rice frittata

You will need about ⅓ cup of uncooked short-grain rice.

1 tablespoon olive oil

2 medium leeks (700g), chopped coarsely

3 slices (45g) prosciutto, chopped finely

7 eggs, beaten lightly

¼ cup (20g) finely grated parmesan cheese

½ cup (125ml) buttermilk

1 cup cooked short-grain white rice

¼ cup finely chopped fresh chives

Heat oil in large saucepan; cook leek and prosciutto, stirring, until leek is soft. Combine leek mixture with remaining ingredients in large bowl. **Pour** mixture into oiled deep 19cm square cake pan; bake, uncovered, in moderate oven about 35 minutes or until browned lightly and set. Stand for 5 minutes before turning out.

tuna slice

1 cup (200g) long-grain white rice

50g butter

1 large brown onion (200g), chopped finely

4 eggs

1 teaspoon gluten-free mild curry powder

1½ cups (185g) coarsely grated cheddar cheese

2 x 180g cans tuna in brine

1¼ cups (310ml) milk

1 teaspoon gluten-free Dijon mustard

2 tablespoons finely chopped fresh parsley

Oil 20cm x 30cm lamington pan, line base and sides with baking paper, extending paper 3cm above edge of pan.

Cook rice in large saucepan of boiling water, uncovered, until just tender; drain, rinse under cold water, drain again. Melt butter in small saucepan; cook onion, stirring, until soft.

Combine rice, half of the onion, one of the eggs, curry powder and one-third of the cheese in large bowl; mix well. Press mixture into prepared pan.

Strain tuna over small bowl; reserve brine. Sprinkle flaked tuna over rice mixture; top with the remaining onion and cheese. Combine reserved brine, milk, mustard and parsley with remaining three eggs in large jug; mix well. Pour egg mixture over tuna mixture; bake, uncovered, in moderate oven about 50 minutes or until firm. Stand slice 5 minutes before cutting.

warm thai beef salad

700g beef rump steak, sliced thinly

1 tablespoon grated fresh ginger

1 tablespoon finely grated lime rind

1 tablespoon lime juice

4 birdseye chillies, seeded, chopped finely

2 tablespoons finely chopped fresh lemon grass

1/4 cup coarsely chopped fresh coriander leaves

250g rice vermicelli

2 tablespoons peanut oil

1 medium brown onion (150g), sliced

1 medium red capsicum (200g), chopped finely

1 Lebanese cucumber (130g), seeded, chopped finely

4 green onions, sliced

lemon mint dressing

1/2 cup (125ml) peanut oil

1/3 cup (80ml) lemon juice

1/4 cup finely chopped fresh mint leaves

2 cloves garlic, crushed

2 teaspoons sugar

Combine beef, ginger, rind, juice, chilli, lemon grass and half of the coriander in large bowl, cover; refrigerate 3 hours or overnight.
Place vermicelli in medium heatproof bowl, cover with boiling water, stand until just tender; drain.
Heat oil in wok or large frying pan; stir-fry beef mixture and brown onion, in batches, until beef is browned and cooked as desired.
Gently toss vermicelli and beef mixture in large bowl with capsicum, cucumber, green onion, remaining coriander and Lemon Mint Dressing.
Lemon Mint Dressing Combine ingredients in jar; shake well.

herb polenta

4 (600g) beef
rib-eye steaks

2 cloves garlic,
crushed

1 tablespoon gluten-
free seeded mustard

2 teaspoons olive oil

tomato herb polenta
2 teaspoons olive oil

1 medium brown onion
(150g), sliced thinly

1.5 litres (6 cups) water

1 large gluten-free
chicken stock cube

400g can tomatoes

1½ cups (250g)
polenta

⅓ cup (25g) finely
grated parmesan
cheese

2 tablespoons
chopped fresh oregano
leaves

Brush steaks on both sides with combined
garlic, mustard and oil. Char-grill (or grill or
barbecue) steaks, until browned both sides
and cooked as desired. Serve with Tomato
Herb Polenta.

Tomato Herb Polenta Heat oil in large
saucepan; cook onion, stirring, until soft.
Add water, crumbled stock cube and
undrained crushed tomatoes; bring to a boil.
Gradually add polenta; simmer, stirring,
about 10 minutes or until polenta thickens.
Stir in cheese and oregano.

orange syrup cake

185g butter

1 tablespoon finely grated orange rind

1¼ cups (275g) caster sugar

6 eggs

3 cups (375g) almond meal

¾ cup (65g) desiccated coconut

¾ cup (110g) rice flour

1 teaspoon gluten-free baking powder

orange syrup

1 large orange (300g)

⅓ cup (75g) caster sugar

⅓ cup (80ml) water

Grease 21cm baba pan. Beat butter, rind and sugar in medium bowl with electric mixer until light and fluffy. Add eggs, one at a time, beating until just combined between additions (mixture will curdle). **Stir** in almond meal, coconut and sifted flour and baking powder. Spread cake mixture into prepared pan; bake in moderate oven about 1 hour. Stand cake in pan 5 minutes; turn onto wire rack over tray. Pour hot Orange Syrup over hot cake; serve warm or cold.

Orange Syrup Using vegetable peeler; peel rind thinly from orange, cut rind into thin strips. Squeeze juice from orange (you need ⅓ cup/80ml) into small saucepan; stir in rind, sugar and water. Stir over heat, without boiling, until sugar dissolves. Simmer, uncovered, without stirring, 5 minutes.

42 thai pork with noodles

500g fresh rice noodles

2 tablespoons peanut oil

500g pork fillets,
sliced thinly

200g oyster
mushrooms, sliced

500g spinach, trimmed

1/4 cup (60ml)
wheat-free tamari

1 tablespoon fish sauce

1 tablespoon sugar

2 teaspoons
sambal oelek

1 tablespoon finely
chopped fresh
coriander leaves

Place noodles in medium heatproof bowl,
cover with boiling water, stand until just
tender; drain.

Heat oil in large frying pan; cook pork, in
batches, until browned all over. Return pork to
pan with mushrooms, spinach leaves, sauces,
sugar and sambal; cook, stirring, until heated
through. Add noodles and coriander; stir
gently until hot.

fiery spanish corn
and bacon rice

2 trimmed corn cobs (500g)

1/4 cup (60ml) olive oil

7 medium egg tomatoes (500g), halved

1 medium green capsicum (200g), sliced thinly

6 bacon rashers, chopped finely

1 medium brown onion (150g), chopped finely

2 cloves garlic, crushed

1 teaspoon cayenne pepper

1 teaspoon hot paprika

1 1/2 teaspoons sambal oelek

2 cups (400g) long-grain white rice

1.25 litres (5 cups) chicken stock

1 bunch fresh chives, trimmed, halved

Cut corn into thick chunks. Boil, steam or microwave corn until just tender; drain. Heat 2 tablespoons of the oil in grill pan; cook corn, tomato and capsicum, in batches, until browned lightly and tender. Cook bacon in same pan until crisp. Cover vegetables, tomato and bacon to keep warm.

Heat remaining oil in large saucepan; cook onion and garlic, stirring, until onion is browned lightly. Add cayenne pepper, paprika, sambal and rice; cook, stirring, 2 minutes. Add 1 litre of the boiling stock; simmer, covered, 12 minutes. Add remaining boiling stock; simmer, covered, until rice is tender and most of the liquid is absorbed. Combine rice with vegetables, tomato and bacon in large bowl, top with chives.

polenta wedges
with ratatouille

3 cups (750ml)
vegetable stock

1 cup (250ml) water

1 cup (170g) polenta

1/2 cup (40g) coarsely
grated romano cheese

1/4 cup (60ml) olive oil

1 large brown onion
(200g), sliced thickly

2 medium red
capsicums (400g)

3 medium
zucchini (360g)

400g can tomatoes

1/4 cup (60ml)
tomato paste

2 tablespoons bottled
gluten-free basil pesto

Bring stock and water to a boil in large saucepan, gradually add polenta;
simmer, stirring, about 10 minutes or until polenta thickens. Stir in cheese.
Press polenta into oiled 22cm round sandwich cake pan; cover, refrigerate
30 minutes or until set.

Heat 1 tablespoon of the oil in large saucepan; cook onion, stirring, until
just soft. Halve capsicums, remove and discard seeds and membranes.
Cut capsicum and zucchini into long, 1cm-wide strips; add to pan with
the undrained crushed tomatoes, paste and pesto. Bring to a boil; simmer,
uncovered, until vegetables are tender.

Meanwhile, turn polenta onto board; cut into eight wedges. Heat remaining
oil in large non-stick frying pan; cook polenta wedges, in batches, until
browned both sides. Serve polenta wedges with ratatouille.

mexicali bean and
rice pie

2 cups (400g) calrose white rice

1¼ cups (310ml) water

1½ cups (375ml) beef stock

1 egg, beaten lightly

2 cups (250g) coarsely grated cheddar cheese

450g can refried beans

1½ cups (375ml) bottled tomato pasta sauce

1 medium tomato (190g), chopped finely

6 green onions, sliced finely

⅔ cup (160ml) sour cream

Place rice, the water and stock in large saucepan. Bring to a boil; simmer, covered, about 15 minutes or until rice is tender and liquid absorbed. Transfer rice to large bowl; cool. Stir in egg and half of the cheese.

Using wet hands, press rice mixture evenly into oiled 34cm pizza pan; bake, uncovered, in moderate oven about 40 minutes or until browned lightly.

Place beans in medium bowl; stir until smooth. Spread rice base with sauce; sprinkle with half of the remaining cheese. Spread with beans; sprinkle with half of the combined tomato and onion, then the remaining cheese. Bake, uncovered, in hot oven about 20 minutes or until cheese melts and pie is heated through. Top with sour cream and remaining tomato and onion.

baked chicken,
kumara and spinach

250g fetta cheese

250g packet frozen spinach, thawed

2 large kumara (1kg), sliced thinly

4 (680g) single chicken breast fillets, sliced thinly

1 large white onion (200g), chopped finely

2 teaspoons finely chopped fresh thyme

1/4 cup (60ml) light sour cream

1/2 cup (125ml) chicken stock

2 teaspoons 100% corn cornflour

1 tablespoon water

2 cups (200g) coarsely grated mozzarella cheese

Crumble fetta into medium bowl. Using hands, squeeze excess moisture from spinach; mix spinach with fetta.

Boil, steam or microwave kumara until just tender; drain.

Meanwhile, cook chicken, in batches, in medium heated oiled frying pan until just cooked through and browned all over. Cook onion and thyme in same pan, stirring, until onion is soft; stir into fetta mixture.

Cook cream, stock and blended flour and water in same pan, stirring, until mixture boils and thickens.

Place half of the kumara, half of the chicken and all of the fetta mixture, in layers, in oiled 3-litre (12-cup) ovenproof dish.

Repeat layering with remaining kumara and chicken; pour cream mixture over the top. Sprinkle with mozzarella; bake, uncovered, in moderately hot oven about 30 minutes or until cheese melts and is browned lightly.

beef rissoles

You will need about ¼ cup of uncooked long-grain brown rice.

20g butter

2 cloves garlic, crushed

1 medium brown onion (150g), chopped finely

2 bacon rashers, chopped finely

500g minced beef

½ cup cooked long-grain brown rice

1 tablespoon milk

rice flour

vegetable oil, for shallow-frying

Melt butter in medium saucepan; cook garlic, onion and bacon, stirring, until onion is soft, cool.

Combine onion mixture with beef, rice and milk in medium bowl; mix well. Divide mixture into eight rissoles. Toss rissoles in flour; shake off excess.

Shallow-fry rissoles, in hot oil, until browned all over and cooked through; drain on absorbent paper.

fruit cake

250g butter, softened

2 teaspoons finely grated orange rind

1 cup (200g) firmly packed brown sugar

2 tablespoons golden syrup

4 eggs

1½ cups (250g) sultanas

1½ cups (250g) chopped raisins

1 cup (160g) chopped seeded dates

¾ cup (110g) dried currants

½ cup (75g) chopped dried apricots

1 cup (125g) almond meal

1¼ cups (185g) gluten-free plain flour

2 teaspoons mixed spice

½ cup (80g) blanched whole almonds

¼ cup (60ml) brandy

Line base and sides of a deep 19cm square or 22cm round cake pan with one layer of brown paper and three layers of baking paper, extending paper 5cm above edge of pan.
Beat butter, rind and sugar in small bowl with electric mixer until just combined. Add golden syrup, then eggs, one at a time, beating until just combined between additions (mixture will curdle).
Transfer mixture to a large bowl, stir in fruit, almond meal, sifted flour and spice.
Spread cake mixture into prepared pan; decorate top with blanched almonds. Bake, uncovered, in slow oven about 3¼ hours. Brush hot cake with brandy, cover tightly with foil; cool in pan.

50 spicy minted
meatballs

You will need about 1/3 cup uncooked basmati rice.

2 cloves garlic, crushed

3 bacon rashers, chopped finely

1 small brown onion (80g), chopped finely

1 cup cooked basmati rice

500g minced beef

1 tablespoon wheat-free tamari

2 teaspoons fish sauce

2 teaspoons ground cumin

1 tablespoon peanut oil

2 x 400g cans tomatoes

2 birdseye chillies, chopped finely

1/4 cup (35g) roasted peanuts, chopped finely

3/4 cup (180ml) coconut milk

1/4 cup finely chopped fresh mint leaves

Cook garlic, bacon and onion in large frying pan, stirring, until onion is soft. Combine onion mixture in large bowl with rice, beef, sauces and cumin. Shape level tablespoons of mixture into balls, place on tray, cover; refrigerate 30 minutes.

Heat oil in same pan; cook meatballs, in batches, until browned. Return meatballs to pan with undrained crushed tomatoes, chilli and peanuts; cook, stirring gently, until meatballs are cooked through. Stir in milk and mint; cook, stirring, until hot (do not boil). Serve with extra boiled rice sprinkled with parsley, if desired.

chicken pilaf
with apricots

60g ghee

1kg chicken thigh fillets, chopped

2 medium brown onions (300g), sliced finely

1 clove garlic, crushed

1 teaspoon ground cumin

1 teaspoon ground coriander

1/2 teaspoon ground turmeric

1/2 cup (75g) dried apricots, sliced finely

2 cups (400g) basmati rice

1 litre (4 cups) chicken stock

1/4 cup (35g) dried currants

1/2 cup (60g) frozen peas

1/2 cup (80g) pine nuts, toasted

Heat half of the ghee in large saucepan; cook chicken, in batches, until browned all over and cooked through, drain on absorbent paper. Heat remaining ghee in same pan; cook onion, garlic and spices, stirring, until onion is soft.

Add apricots and rice, stir over heat until rice is coated in spice mixture. Stir in stock; simmer, covered with tight-fitting lid, 15 minutes. Remove from heat, stir in chicken; stand, covered, 15 minutes. Stir in currants, peas and nuts. Top with chopped fresh coriander, if desired.

You will need about 1¹/₃ cups uncooked long-grain rice.

4 cups cooked long-grain white rice

20g butter

1 cup (125g) coarsely grated cheddar cheese

2 tablespoons finely grated parmesan cheese

1 egg, beaten lightly

1 tablespoon finely chopped fresh flat-leaf parsley

filling

500g lamb neck chops

1 tablespoon vegetable oil

1 small brown onion (80g), chopped finely

1 small carrot (70g), sliced finely

¹/₂ trimmed stick celery (40g), sliced finely

100g flat mushrooms, chopped finely

¹/₂ cup (125ml) chicken stock

400g can tomatoes

1¹/₂ tablespoons 100% corn cornflour

1 tablespoon water

1 tablespoon finely chopped fresh flat-leaf parsley

Combine warm rice with butter, cheeses and egg in large bowl; mix well. Press ³/₄ cup of the rice mixture over base and sides of four 11cm oiled pie dishes (1 cup/250ml).

Spread Filling into rice shells. Press remaining rice around edge of each dish, leaving a 2cm circle in the centre. Place pies on oven tray; bake, uncovered, in moderately hot oven about 40 minutes or until browned. Sprinkle centres with parsley.

Filling Remove bones from lamb, cut lamb into 1cm pieces. Heat oil in large saucepan; cook lamb and onion, stirring, until lamb is browned. Add carrot, celery and mushrooms; cook, covered, until vegetables are tender. Stir in stock and undrained crushed tomatoes; simmer, covered, about 45 minutes or until lamb is tender. Add blended cornflour and water, stir over heat until mixture boils and thickens. Stir in parsley.

oregano chicken
with cheesy rice topping

You will need about 1/2 cup uncooked long-grain rice.

4 (680g) single chicken breast fillets

2 cloves garlic, crushed

2 tablespoons lemon juice

1 tablespoon finely chopped fresh oregano leaves

2 tablespoons olive oil

cheesy rice topping

1 1/2 cups cooked long-grain white rice

1 egg yolk

1/3 cup (40g) coarsely grated cheddar cheese

1/3 cup (25g) finely grated parmesan cheese

30g butter

tomato herb sauce

2 teaspoons olive oil

1 clove garlic, crushed

400g can tomatoes

1/4 cup (60ml) dry red wine

1/2 cup (125ml) water

1 teaspoon sugar

1 teaspoon finely chopped fresh oregano leaves

Combine chicken with garlic, juice, oregano and half of the oil in large bowl. Cover; refrigerate 3 hours or overnight.
Heat remaining oil in large frying pan; cook chicken, until browned both sides and cooked through. Spread one side of each warm chicken breast with Cheesy Rice Topping; grill until browned. Serve with Tomato Herb Sauce.
Cheesy Rice Topping Process ingredients until combined.
Tomato Herb Sauce Heat oil in small saucepan; cook garlic until fragrant. Stir in undrained crushed tomatoes and remaining ingredients; simmer, uncovered, until thickened slightly.

grilled vegetable flan

*You will need about
1 cup uncooked calrose
brown rice.*

*2 cups cooked calrose
brown rice*

1 egg, beaten lightly

*½ cup (40g) finely grated
parmesan cheese*

*2 medium red
capsicums (400g)*

*4 medium
zucchini (480g)*

1 tablespoon olive oil

*2 tablespoons bottled
gluten-free basil pesto*

*2 eggs, beaten
lightly, extra*

½ cup (125ml) cream

Process half of the rice until finely
chopped. Combine processed rice,
remaining rice, egg and cheese in
bowl; mix well. Press rice mixture over
base of oiled 23cm shallow pie dish.

Quarter capsicums, remove and discard
seeds and membranes. Roast under grill
or in very hot oven, skin-side up, until
skin blisters and blackens. Cover
capsicum pieces in plastic or paper
for 5 minutes, peel away skin, cut
capsicum into 3cm strips.

Cut zucchini lengthways into 7mm slices,
brush with oil; grill until browned on both
sides. Spread pesto over rice base, top
with capsicum and zucchini. Pour combined
extra eggs and cream over vegetables.
Bake, uncovered, in moderate oven about
35 minutes or until set.

56 eggplant filled
with silverbeet and lentils

4 medium
eggplants (1.2kg)

1½ cups (300g)
brown lentils

2 tablespoons olive oil

1 large brown
onion (200g),
chopped coarsely

1 clove garlic, crushed

400g can tomatoes

1 tablespoon
tomato paste

500g silverbeet,
trimmed

¼ cup coarsely
chopped fresh
coriander leaves

1¼ cups (125g)
coarsely grated
mozzarella cheese

Halve eggplants lengthways; place in oiled baking dish. Bake, uncovered, in very hot oven about 15 minutes or until just tender.

Scoop out flesh from eggplant, leaving a 5mm shell; chop flesh coarsely.

Add lentils to medium saucepan of boiling water; boil, uncovered, about 15 minutes or until tender, drain.

Heat oil in large saucepan; cook onion and garlic, stirring, until onion is soft. Add eggplant flesh, lentils, undrained crushed tomatoes, paste and coarsely chopped silverbeet; cook, stirring, until silverbeet is just wilted. Stir in coriander.

Divide lentil mixture among eggplant shells; sprinkle with cheese. Bake, uncovered, in moderate oven about 30 minutes or until browned.

sweet chilli vegetable, noodle and tofu stir-fry

300g firm tofu

375g dried rice
stick noodles

1/4 cup (60ml)
peanut oil

2 medium brown
onions (300g),
sliced thinly

2 cloves garlic,
crushed

200g button
mushrooms,
sliced thinly

300g baby bok choy,
chopped coarsely

1 tablespoon
white vinegar

1/2 cup (125ml) sweet
chilli sauce

100g tat soi

Cut tofu into 2cm cubes; drain tofu on absorbent paper.
Place noodles in large heatproof bowl, cover with boiling water,
stand only until just tender; drain.
Heat 2 tablespoons of the oil in wok or large frying pan; stir-fry tofu,
in batches, until browned lightly. Drain on absorbent paper. Heat
remaining oil in same wok; stir-fry onion and garlic until onion is soft. Add
mushrooms; stir-fry until mushrooms are tender. Add bok choy, noodles,
vinegar and sauce; stir-fry until hot. Add tat soi; stir-fry until tat soi is
barely wilted. Toss tofu gently through mixture; serve immediately.

58 polenta burgers

You will need about ¹/₄ cup of uncooked short-grain rice.

1 litre (4 cups) water

1 cup (170g) polenta

1 cup (125g) coarsely grated cheddar cheese

rice flour

vegetable oil, for shallow-frying

2 tablespoons vegetable oil, extra

1 small zucchini (90g), sliced thinly

1 small eggplant (230g), sliced thinly

1 small brown onion (80g), sliced thinly

1 small tomato (130g), sliced thinly

patties

³/₄ cup cooked short-grain white rice

200g minced beef

³/₄ cup (65g) stale gluten-free breadcrumbs

1 teaspoon dried basil leaves

1 tablespoon tomato paste

Bring the water to a boil in large saucepan; gradually add polenta, simmer, stirring, about 10 minutes or until polenta thickens. Stir in cheese. Press polenta into oiled 26cm x 32cm Swiss roll pan, refrigerate until set. Cut polenta into eight pieces, toss in flour; shake off excess. Shallow-fry polenta, in hot oil, until browned all over; drain on absorbent paper.

Heat extra oil in large frying pan; cook zucchini, eggplant and onion, in batches, until softened, remove from pan. Cook Patties in same pan, until browned both sides and cooked through. Serve Patties, tomato and vegetables between polenta pieces.

Patties Combine ingredients in medium bowl. Shape into four patties, refrigerate 30 minutes.

creamy beef

and mushrooms

40g butter

500g beef rump steak, sliced thinly

1 medium brown onion (150g), chopped finely

2 cloves garlic, crushed

200g button mushrooms, halved

1 teaspoon sweet paprika

1 tablespoon lemon juice

2 teaspoons wheat-free tamari

1/2 large gluten-free vegetable stock cube

1/2 cup (125ml) coconut milk

Melt butter in large saucepan; cook beef, in batches, until browned all over.

Cook onion and garlic in same pan, stirring, until onion is soft. Add mushrooms and paprika; cook, stirring, until mushrooms are browned lightly. Return beef to pan with juice, sauce and crumbled stock cube; simmer, covered, about 5 minutes or until beef is tender. Stir in coconut milk, stir until heated through.

Serve with brown rice, if desired.

glossary

allspice also known as pimento.

almond meal almonds ground to flour-like texture.

bacon rashers also known as slices of bacon. Bacon may contain glucose syrup – but is so highly processed that, when tested, it shows no detectable gluten.

baking powder (gluten free) a raising agent available from health food shops.

basil pesto a commercial product consisting of basil, oil, vinegar, garlic, nuts and parmesan (gluten-free – contains no thickeners).

bicarbonate of soda also known as baking soda.

beef mince ground beef.

bok choy also known as pak choi or Chinese white cabbage.

brandy spirit distilled from wine (may contain caramel colour – but contains no detectable gluten).

breadcrumbs

stale gluten-free: made from yeast-free, gluten-free and wheat-free bread.

capers grey-green buds from warm-climate shrub, sold pickled or dried and salted.

chillies available in many different types and sizes. Use rubber gloves when seeding and chopping.

powder: the Asian variety is the hottest; it can be used as a substitute for fresh chillies in the proportion of ½ teaspoon ground chilli powder to 1 medium chopped fresh chilli.

sweet chilli sauce: a mild sauce made from red chillies. It contains MSG which can be derived from wheat, but most is not – when tested shows no detectable gluten.

Chinese cabbage also known as Peking cabbage or wong bok.

cocoa cocoa powder.

cornflour (100% corn) ground grains of corn; buy from some supermarkets and health food shops.

curry powder (gluten-free mild) a blend of ground spices. Many curry powders have gluten – but Clive of India brand is gluten-free.

eggs some recipes call for raw or barely cooked eggs; exercise caution if there is a salmonella problem in your area.

fish sauce also called nam pla or nuoc nam.

flour

buckwheat: available from some supermarkets and health food shops.

plain gluten-free: a mix of maize starch, wholegrain rice, arrowroot/tapioca starch, whole maize and soy flour; available from health food shops.

potato: is made from cooked potatoes, dried and ground.

rice: a very fine flour, made from ground white rice.

rice brown: ground whole-grain brown rice.

soy: made from ground soy beans.

fruche commercial dessert similar to fromage frais.

ghee clarified butter; with the milk solids removed.

jam also known as preserve or conserve.

kumara Polynesian name of orange-fleshed sweet potato often confused with yam.

lemon grass a tall, clumping, lemon-smelling and tasting, sharp-edged grass; the white lower part of each stem is used.

mayonnaise, whole egg we used S & W brand.

mixed spice blend of ground spices (read product labels – some spice blends have wheat starch in them).

mustard

dijon: fairly mild French mustard. Masterfoods Dijon mustard is gluten-free.

seeded: also known as wholegrain; coarse-grain mustard made of crushed mustard seeds and Dijon-style French mustard. Masterfoods Seeded mustard is gluten-free.

noodles

fresh rice: made from rice and vegetable oil.

fresh rice noodle sheets: available from Asian grocery shops.

rice stick: dried noodles, available in packets.

rice vermicelli: also known as rice-flour noodles and rice-stick noodles; made from ground rice and sold dried.

oil

cooking-oil spray: vegetable oil in an aerosol can.

olive: mono-unsaturated; made from the pressing of tree-ripened olives. Extra Light or Light describes the flavour, not the fat levels.

peanut: pressed from ground peanuts.

vegetable: oils sourced from plants instead of animal fats.

onion

green: also known as scallion or (incorrectly) shallot.

red: also known as Spanish, red Spanish or Bermuda onion; large and purple-red.

pasta (wheat and gluten free) available from some supermarkets and health food stores.

polenta a flour-like cereal made of ground corn (maize); also the name of the dish made from it.

pork fillet skinless, boneless eye-fillet cut from the loin.

pork and veal mince a mix of ground pork and veal.

prawns also known as shrimp.

prosciutto salt-cured, air-dried (unsmoked), pressed ham.

puffed rice available from health food stores.

refried beans pinto beans cooked twice: soaked and boiled then mashed and fried, traditionally in lard. Available in supermarkets.

rice all rice is gluten-free.

sambal oelek (also ulek or olek) a salty Indonesian chilli paste.

sausages, gluten-free rice flour is used instead of wheat flour as the binding agent in these sausages.

silverbeet also known as Swiss chard or seakale.

spinach also known as English spinach; has delicate, crinkled green leaves on thin stems.

star anise a star-shaped, dried pod whose seeds have an aniseed flavour.

stock use homemade stock or gluten-free stock cubes.

sugar we used granulated coarse table sugar, also known as crystal sugar, unless otherwise specified.

brown: an extremely soft, fine granulated sugar retaining molasses for its colour and flavour.

caster: also known as superfine or finely granulated table sugar.

sugar snap peas small pods containing formed peas.

sultanas golden raisins.

tamari, wheat-free a sauce made from soy beans.

tandoori paste consisting of garlic, tamarind, ginger, coriander, chilli and spices.

tat soi also known as rosette pak choy, tai gu choy or Chinese flat cabbage.

tofu, firm also known as bean curd; made from the "milk" of crushed soy beans.

yogurt, pure cultured plain unflavoured yogurt.

conversion chart

MEASURES

One Australian metric measuring cup holds approximately 250ml, one Australian metric tablespoon holds 20ml, one Australian metric teaspoon holds 5ml.

The difference between one country's measuring cups and another's is within a 2- or 3-teaspoon variance, and will not affect your cooking results. North America, New Zealand and the United Kingdom use a 15ml tablespoon. All cup and spoon measurements are level. The most accurate way of measuring dry ingredients is to weigh them. When measuring liquids, use a clear glass or plastic jug with metric markings.

We use large eggs with an average weight of 60g.

DRY MEASURES

METRIC	IMPERIAL
15g	½oz
30g	1oz
60g	2oz
90g	3oz
125g	4oz (¼lb)
155g	5oz
185g	6oz
220g	7oz
250g	8oz (½lb)
280g	9oz
315g	10oz
345g	11oz
375g	12oz (¾lb)
410g	13oz
440g	14oz
470g	15oz
500g	16oz (1lb)
750g	24oz (1½lb)
1kg	32oz (2lb)

LIQUID MEASURES

METRIC	IMPERIAL
30ml	1 fluid oz
60ml	2 fluid oz
100ml	3 fluid oz
125ml	4 fluid oz
150ml	5 fluid oz (¼ pint/1 gill)
190ml	6 fluid oz
250ml	8 fluid oz
300ml	10 fluid oz (½ pint)
500ml	16 fluid oz
600ml	20 fluid oz (1 pint)
1000ml (1 litre)	1¾ pints

LENGTH MEASURES

METRIC	IMPERIAL
3mm	⅛in
6mm	¼in
1cm	½in
2cm	¾in
2.5cm	1in
5cm	2in
6cm	2½in
8cm	3in
10cm	4in
13cm	5in
15cm	6in
18cm	7in
20cm	8in
23cm	9in
25cm	10in
28cm	11in
30cm	12in (1ft)

OVEN TEMPERATURES

These oven temperatures are only a guide for conventional ovens.
For fan-forced ovens, check the manufacturer's manual.

	°C (CELSIUS)	°F (FAHRENHEIT)	GAS MARK
Very slow	120	250	½
Slow	150	275 – 300	1 – 2
Moderately slow	160	325	3
Moderate	180	350 – 375	4 – 5
Moderately hot	200	400	6
Hot	220	425 – 450	7 – 8
Very hot	240	475	9

Published in 2001 by Bauer Media Books, Sydney
Bauer Media Books are published by Bauer Media Limited
54 Park St, Sydney
GPO Box 4088, Sydney, NSW 2001.
phone (02) 9282 8618; fax (02) 9126 3702
www.awwcookbooks.com.au

MEDIA GROUP

BAUER MEDIA BOOKS
Publishing Director – Gerry Reynolds
Publisher – Sally Wright
Editorial & Food Director – Pamela Clark
Creative Director – Hieu Chi Nguyen
Food Concept Director – Sophia Young
Director of Sales, Marketing & Rights – Brian Cearnes

Published and Distributed in the United Kingdom by Octopus Publishing Group
Endeavour House
189 Shaftesbury Avenue
London WC2H 8JY
United Kingdom
phone (+44)(0)207 632 5400; fax (+44)(0)207 632 5405
info@octopus-publishing.co.uk;
www.octopusbooks.co.uk

To order books:
telephone LBS on 01903 828 503
order online at
www.australian-womens-weekly.com
or www.octopusbooks.co.uk

Printed in Thailand
International foreign language rights, Brian Cearnes, Bauer Media Books
bcearnes@bauer-media.com.au

A catalogue record for this book is available from the British Library.
ISBN 978-1-90742-899-9
© Bauer Media Limited 2001
ABN 18 053 273 546
First published in 2001. Reprinted 2004, 2006, 2007, 2010.
This edition published in 2013.